Publisher`s Note:
Please note that the German and English versions of the story were written to be as close as possible. However, in some cases they may differ in order to accomodate the nuances and fluidity of each language. Author, translator, and publisher made every effort to ensure accuracy. We therefore take no responsibility for inconsistency and minor errors.

Translated by the author
Illustrations by Supuni Suriyarachchi
Copy design and book layout by Emy Farella

ISBN: 979-8-483173-04-5
1. Edition 2021

INGO BLUM

The FLYING TREE

DER FLIEGENDE BAUM

Illustrated by
Supuni Suriyarachchi

BILINGUAL
ENGLISH | GERMAN

Once on a **hill** there stood a tree.

Auf einem **Hügel** stand einmal ein Baum.

He felt **lonely** and **bored** and wanted **to break free**.

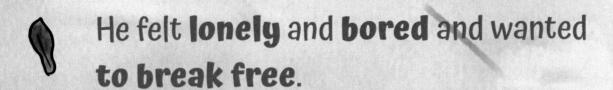

Er fühlte sich **einsam** und **gelangweilt** und **wollte frei sein**.

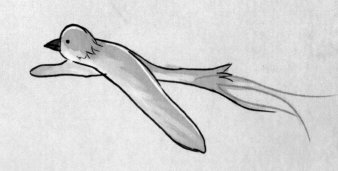

"I wish I could fly up in the **sky** and see the world from above. From this place I want to flee!"

„Ich wünschte, ich könnte in den **Himmel** fliegen und die Welt von oben sehen. Von diesem Ort möchte ich fliehen."

"No animal rests at my solid trunk.

No **bear**, no **deer**, not even a **skunk**."

„Kein Tier ruht an meinem festen Stamm

Kein **Bär**, kein **Hirsch**, nicht einmal ein **Stinktier**."

The spring came, and a swallow sat down on the tree.

"Can you give me shelter?" she asked.

Der Frühling kam, und eine Schwalbe setzte sich auf den Baum.

„Kannst du mir Unterschlupf geben?" fragte sie.

"Sure, **it's all free!**"

„Sicher, **es ist alles umsonst!**"

"This place is so boring", said the tree. "I would love to see some other places."

"I can do magic," the swallow said. "I know a lot of other spaces."

„**Dieser Ort ist langweilig**", sagte der Baum. „Ich würde gerne mal andere Orte sehen."

„**Ich kann zaubern**", sagte die Schwalbe. „Ich kenne viele andere Orte."

Suddenly, the tree felt like he was pulled out of the ground.

Plötzlich fühlte sich der Baum, als ob er aus dem Boden gezogen würde.

All with his roots, with a cracking sound. He was lifted up in the sky and heard the swallow cry, "Use your **branches** to **move** and **fly!**"

Mit all seinen **Wurzeln**, mit einem knackenden Geräusch. Er wurde in den Himmel emporgehoben und hörte die Schwalbe rufen: „Benutze deine **Äste**, um dich zu **bewegen** und zu **fliegen!**"

The other trees stood in wonder, whispering "**Come back soon!**"

The tree was very fast, hovering like a wonderful balloon.

Die anderen Bäume standen staunend da und flüsterten: „**Komm bald wieder!**" Der Baum war schnell, er schwebte wie ein wunderbarer Ballon.

They flew over lakes, and forests,
and villages and over a cloud.

The tree cried "**yoo-hoo**", very loud.

Sie flogen über Seen und Wälder und
Dörfer und über eine Wolke.
Der Baum rief sehr laut „**Juhu**!"

Soon they came **into a fog**
and could not see.

The tree was exhausted,
but enjoyed **to be free**.

Bald kamen sie **in einen Nebel**
und konnten nichts mehr sehen.

Der Baum war erschöpft,
aber froh, **frei zu sein**.

"Do you like what you see," the swallow asked.
They looked back to a hill they just passed.

„Gefällt dir, was du siehst?", fragte die Schwalbe.

Sie blickten zurück zu einem Hügel, an dem sie gerade vorbeigekommen waren.

The tree nodded happily, but needed a rest. He wished he could **build something** like a swallow's nest.

Der Baum nickte freudig, brauchte aber eine Pause. Er wünschte sich, er könnte auch so **etwas wie ein Schwalbennest bauen.**

When they landed on a mountain,
it was much **too cold**. The tree did not like
that. The place was **odd** and **old**.

Als sie auf einem Berg landeten, war es viel
zu kalt. Das gefiel dem Baum nicht.
Der Ort war **seltsam** und **alt**.

They carried on and came to a **big city**.

They saw some trees that didn't look very happy.

Sie flogen weiter und kamen in eine **große Stadt**.

Sie sahen einige Bäume, die nicht sehr glücklich aussahen.

"I want to see more," the tree **whooped** with joy.

And made some somersaults in the air, like a **little boy**.

„Ich will noch mehr sehen", **jubelte** der Baum vor Freude.

Und er machte einige Purzelbäume in der Luft, wie ein **kleiner Junge**.

They came to a desert which was very **hot**, a very dry spot!

Sie kamen in eine Wüste, die sehr **heiß** war, ein sehr trockener Ort!

In a **forest** they heard a loud, roaring **noise**.

In einem **Wald** hörten sie ein lautes, dröhnendes Geräusch.

They saw some loggers, with chainsaws,
one was shouting in an **angry voice**.

Sie sahen einige Holzfäller mit Kettensägen,
einer schrie mit **wütender Stimme**.

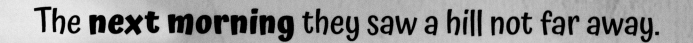

The **next morning** they saw a hill not far away.

Am **nächsten Morgen** sahen sie nicht weit entfernt einen Hügel.

"**This is my hill,**" the tree suddenly cried, "this is my hood!"

„**Das ist mein Hügel**", rief der Baum fröhlich, „das ist meine Heimat!"

Slowly he moved his **roots** to the hole, adjusting with care.

Langsam bewegte er seine **Wurzeln** in das Loch und passte sie vorsichtig an.

"There is no place like home!
I don't want to be like the birds."

„Es gibt keinen Ort wie Zuhause!
Ich will nicht wie die Vögel sein."

The little swallow nodded and smiled.
She has always known.

You leave a **big** hole when
you are leaving home.

Die kleine Schwalbe nickte und lächelte.
Sie hat es immer gewusst.

Man hinterlässt ein **großes** Loch,
wenn man seine Heimat verläßt.

pics TO COLOR

More Bilingual Books

ISBN **979-8672025681**

ISBN **979-8682547906**

ISBN **979-8460931347**

ISBN **978-1983093975**

Made in the USA
Middletown, DE
11 September 2024

60825990R00035